Carman Ministries

📖
Harrison House
Tulsa, Oklahoma

6th Printing
Over 229,000 in Print

Radically Saved
ISBN 0-89274-638-6
Copyright © 1993 by Carman Ministries Inc.
P. O. Box 5093
Brentwood, TN 37024-5093

Published by Harrison House, Inc.
P. O. Box 35035
Tulsa, Oklahoma 74153

CONTENTS

1

Radically Saved!

Congratulations! You have made the most important and exciting decision of your life. There is nothing more wonderful than establishing a personal relationship with God. Your commitment of heart and life to Christ has made this relationship possible. By committing your life to Jesus Christ as your Savior and Lord and turning from your sins, you have become a new creation.

You are living proof that the age of miracles has not ended, because the miracle of new birth has happened to you. This commitment is so life-transforming that Jesus referred to it as being *born again*. Born-again is one of several expressions the Bible uses in reference to your experience of coming to know Jesus Christ in a personal way. Your first birth was a physical birth, and now you also have experienced a spiritual birth. Jesus said, **That which is born of the flesh is flesh, and that which is born of the Spirit is spirit.**

Do not marvel that I said to you, "**You must be born again**" (John 3:6,7). Now, not only is your body alive; your spirit and inner person are alive as well. You have become **alive to God in Christ Jesus our Lord** (Romans 6:11).

The Bible also refers to your new condition of being in Christ as being *saved*. You have been saved from the wages or penalties of your sins, which is being eternally without God and without hope. Right now, those without Christ live under condemnation for their sins. Jesus, in reference to Himself, said, **He who believes in Him is not condemned; but he who does not believe is condemned already, because he has not believed in the name of the only begotten Son of God** (John 3:18).

No one denies that every person has committed some wrong. The Bible clearly says, **All have sinned and fall short of the glory of God** (Romans 3:23). However, sin must be paid for, and the punishment for sin is death and separation from God. You can pay for your sins yourself or trust that when Jesus shed His blood for you, He made the payment for you. The Bible says, **The wages of sin is death, but the gift of God is eternal life in Christ Jesus our Lord** (Romans 6:23).

Now that you have put your faith and confidence in Jesus making your payment, you will be saved from the terrible day when God judges the unbeliever for his sin and unbelief. This is when Jesus will return.

In flaming fire taking vengeance on those who do not know God, and on those who do not obey the gospel of our Lord Jesus Christ. These shall be punished with everlasting destruction from the presence of the Lord and from the glory of His power, when He comes, in that Day, to be glorified in His saints and to be admired among all those who believe...

2 Thessalonians 1:8-10

The Bible gives us this assurance, **That if you confess with your mouth the Lord Jesus and believe in your heart that God has raised Him from the dead, you will be**

saved (Romans 10:9). Have you done that? Have you confessed the living Christ as your Savior? If you have, the Bible says salvation is yours!

Don't forget, it is God who does the saving. We benefit from the work He has already done. **Not by works of righteousness which we have done, but according to His mercy He saved us, through the washing of regeneration and renewing of the Holy Spirit** (Titus 3:5).

The Bible also declares that you have been *redeemed* — redeemed from the control of Satan and sin. Webster's Dictionary defines the word *redeemed* as, "freed from captivity by payment of ransom." You were purchased by the blood of Jesus Christ.

Knowing that you were not redeemed with corruptible things, like silver or gold, from your aimless conduct received by tradition from your fathers, but with the precious blood of Christ, as a lamb without blemish and without spot.

1 Peter 1:18, 19

Since Christ purchased you with His blood, He is your rightful owner. One of His rights as your owner is that He has freedom to control every area of your life. Imagine that you bought a house. After you finish the purchasing process, the previous owner tells you that he still owns the living room, the master bedroom and the garage. What would you say? You would probably tell him, "Hey, I paid the full price for this house. I have the right to demand every room!" It is the same with Christ. He paid the full price for you, and now He has the right to demand the full product of your life. Don't hold anything back from His gracious control. Since He created you, He knows best how you should live. **For you were bought at a price; therefore glorify God in your body and in your spirit, which are God's** (1 Corinthians 6:20).

Understand this, the Bible says that you have been *converted*. That means you have been changed. Once you were lost, now you are saved. Once you were separated from God, now you are His child. Once you were on the road to hell, now you are going to heaven. Once you thought you could make it on your own, now you know that you need Jesus. That is why Jesus said, . . .**unless you are converted and become as little children, you will by no means enter the kingdom of heaven** (Matthew 18:3).

You Can Be Sure

One of the most crippling attacks that the devil hurls at new Christians is his attempt to make them doubt their salvation. "Maybe I didn't say the right things." "What if I wasn't sincere enough?" "Can I really live the Christian life?" "What if I sin?" Satan tries to haunt people with these and a thousand other little barbs of doubt.

But, thank God, there is a way to full assurance. You need never doubt your salvation. You don't have to succumb to fear or doubt.

Remember this: *Your ultimate assurance of salvation is in the fact that Jesus Christ lives inside of you.* Since you have made this commitment of your life to Christ, the Bible says that Christ now lives in you. Jesus has made a wonderful promise to all who receive Him. He promised, **Behold, I stand at the door** [of your life] **and knock. If anyone hears My voice and opens the door, I will come in to him. . .** (Revelation 3:20).

Have you done that? Have you opened the door of your life to Jesus? If so, where is Jesus? He has come to live inside of you! That is His promise to you. Just think of it! Jesus Christ actually lives inside of you by His Spirit. His life inside of you is your guarantee of salvation and eternal life. The Bible says, **And this is the testimony: that God has given us eternal life, and this life is in His Son. He who has the Son has life; he who does not have the Son of God does not have life** (1 John 5:11, 12).

"But," you may say, "you don't know some of the terrible things I have done. How can God accept me after what I have done?" God doesn't accept you on the basis of what you have or have not done. He accepts you on the basis of what He has done. He accepts you because Christ, the Holy One, lives in you. Christ is in you and you are in Christ. When you receive Christ as your Lord and Savior, you are put in the protective place of being *in Christ.* God accepts you because Christ is in you and because you are in Christ. The Bible says that **He** [Jesus Christ] **has made us accepted in the Beloved** (Ephesians 1:6).

The devil knows that you will never grow much in your walk with Christ if you constantly fear that your salvation is in jeopardy. But don't let him defeat you with doubts. You are not on probation with God. He has not only given you life, He has given you eternal life. You have been born into His family and you cannot be *un-birthed.* You have **been born again, not of corruptible seed but incorruptible, through the word of God which lives and abides forever** (1 Peter 1:23).

The Bible is clear that you are saved by the grace of God. This means that God, because of His infinite love, saves you when you put your trust in Christ, even though you do not merit or deserve His favor. **For by grace you have been saved through faith, and that not of yourselves; it is the gift of God, not of works, lest anyone should boast** (Ephesians 2:8, 9).

When you get to heaven, you will not see anyone boasting about how they deserve to be there because of their good life. They will know they are there purely because of God's amazing grace. In gratitude to God for His wonderful salvation, you will want to live a life that is pleasing to Him. **For the grace of God that brings salvation has appeared to all men, teaching us that, denying ungodliness and worldly lusts, we should live soberly, righteously, and godly in the present age** (Titus 2:11,12).

If you are plagued with doubt from time to time, here are three simple steps to your assurance of salvation:

1) *Salvation is not your accomplishment but His accomplishment.* As the old hymn says, "Jesus paid it all/All to Him I owe." What more could be added to the blood that

Jesus has spilt for you? You must be persuaded, as Paul was, that Jesus is perfectly capable of protecting and keeping what He has purchased . . .**for I know whom I have believed and am persuaded that He is able to keep what I have committed to Him until that Day** (2 Timothy 1:12).

God does the saving. Therefore, your salvation does not depend upon your strength but upon His strength. Salvation is not something you do, it is something God has done for you. All the religions of the world begin with do's and don'ts. But biblical Christianity begins with *done!* On the cross Jesus cried, *It is finished!* The price for your salvation has been paid in full. Now you can know you are saved, not only because you have given your life to Jesus, but because Jesus has given His life for you.

2) *Trust God's promises to you.* God is perfect in all His ways. Therefore, God not only will not lie to you, the Bible says He cannot lie. Because of your faith in Christ, you now have **eternal life which God, who**

cannot lie, **promised before time began** (Titus 1:2).

No man has ever been as trustworthy as Jesus Christ. And it is Jesus Himself who has promised, **Most assuredly, I say to you, he who hears My word and believes in Him who sent Me has everlasting life, and shall not come into judgment, but has passed from death into life** (John 5:24).

Again, He has promised, **I am the door. If anyone enters by Me, he will be saved, and will go in and out and find pasture** (John 10:9).

Still again He has assured you, **And I give them eternal life, and they shall never perish; neither shall anyone snatch them out of My hand. My Father, who has given them to Me, is greater than all; and no one is able to snatch them out of My Father's hand** (John 10:28, 29).

And still another time He promises, **I will never leave you nor forsake you** (Hebrews 13:5).

So put your confidence in God, who cannot lie, and in His word which endures forever.

3) ***Don't trust your feelings.*** Perhaps the two most changeable things in life are the weather and human emotions. One minute you can be on the mountain top of exhilaration and the next minute in the valley of despair. Many times our emotions are subject to the circumstances that surround us. How tragic, then, if your faith is in how you feel at any particular moment rather than in God. Your hope of salvation simply cannot rest on how you feel at any given moment. Rather, your hope of eternal life must be squarely planted in a settled fact of history — that Jesus Christ died for you and rose again.

There will be times when your heart thrills at the presence of Jesus. This is a good thing. Your faith should not be void of emotion. Any relationship has emotions tied in with it and you have entered into a relationship with Jesus. Simply put, do not depend on your feelings for the assurance of salvation. So when in doubt, doubt your doubts and trust the promises of God.

You Are a New Person

The growth rate of every Christian is different. Some new believers seem to grow rapidly while others seem to grow slowly but surely. You can be certain of this: You *will* grow. Every created thing, both in the plant kingdom and in the animal kingdom, grows if it is alive. So it is with you. You have been made alive in Jesus Christ. And because there is new life in you, you will grow.

Already, you may be discovering something fascinating and exciting happening to you. You are beginning to think differently. You are beginning to act differently. Things you once hated, you now love. Things you once loved, you now despise. Whereas once you were tolerant and accepting of sin, now you despise it. Whereas once you were indifferent or even hostile to spiritual things, now you **hunger and thirst for righteousness** (Matthew 5:6). Indeed, you are a new person. **Therefore, if anyone is in Christ, he is a new creation; old things have passed away, behold, all things have become new.** (2 Corinthians 5:17).

Not only have you changed, you are continuing to be changed. God will continue His work in your life. God's ultimate purpose in bringing you into His family is to have fellowship with you, while molding you into His image.

A wonderful transaction takes place the moment you come to Christ. God forgives your sin. **And you, being dead in your trespasses and in the uncircumcision of your flesh** [old way of living], **He has made alive together with Him, having forgiven you all trespasses** (Colossians 2:13).

God puts His righteousness in you, **even the righteousness of God which is through faith in Jesus Christ to all and on all who believe** (Romans 3:22). God makes you forever His child. **But as many as received Him, to them He gave the right to become children of God, even to those who believe in His name** (John 1:12).

You Have a New Destiny

God has taken you on as a life-time project. From now on, you will be aware of His presence in your life, always seeking to bless you, strengthen you and conform you into the very image of Christ. Your life will continue to have its problems, but you have met the problem-solver.

Some people seem to have the idea that, if a person becomes a Christian, all the joy and excitement will be stripped out of life. This is one of the devil's most ridiculous lies because nothing could be further from the truth. When a person comes to Christ, that's when the excitement really begins. A non-Christian seeks joy and, at best, only finds surface happiness. But a Christian in fellowship with His Lord has the deep-seated joy of knowing that he has found meaning for his life. He has the unspeakable peace of knowing that his sins are forgiven and covered by the blood of Christ. He has the profound thrill of knowing that He is a participant in God's lofty purposes in the earth.

Because Christ is in you, you have the promise of abundant life now and eternal life with Him in heaven. Jesus said, **The thief** [the devil] **does not come except to steal, and to kill, and to destroy. I have come that they may have life, and that they may have it more abundantly** (John 10:10). As you live in fellowship with Christ, your life will be full, meaningful and abundant.

In Christ, you have both abundant life and eternal life. Eternal life means that you will live forever with the Lord in heaven. But to have eternal life also means that you have the very life of God living in you. The life of God, the uncreated One without beginning and without end, is now in you.

So welcome to the family of God! The Almighty God has staked His claim on you. He will continue His loving, transforming work in you until all of His designs for you and through you are completed. Count on it.

Being confident of this very thing, that He who has begun a good work in you will complete it until the day of Jesus Christ.

Philippians 1:6

2

Who Is the Holy Spirit?

"A person can breathe without air as easily as a Christian can live without the Holy Spirit." These forceful words by nineteenth-century evangelist D. L. Moody clearly remind us of our need of the presence and power of the Holy Spirit.

The Holy Spirit is God actively involved in our world today. Jesus referred to the Holy Spirit as the *Comforter* that He would send to help us and encourage us. When you received Christ as your Lord and Savior, the Holy Spirit came to reside in you. It is the Holy Spirit who gives us the power to live a life that is pleasing to God.

The Ministry of the Holy Spirit

The central work of the Holy Spirit is to point people to Jesus Christ. Before you came to Christ, the Holy Spirit was actively drawing you to Him. Since you have been saved, the

Holy Spirit continues to work, from the inside, to keep you centered on the Lord Jesus.

It is the Holy Spirit who convicts the non-Christian of his need for Christ. Concerning this work of the Spirit, Jesus said, **And when He has come, He will convict the world of sin, and of righteousness, and of judgment** (John 16:8).

It is the Holy Spirit who guides believers into an ever-deepening relationship with the Lord. Jesus said, **When He, the Spirit of truth, has come, He will guide you into all truth; for He will not speak on His own authority, but whatever He hears He will speak; and He will tell you things to come. He will glorify me, for He will take of what is Mine and declare it to you** (John 16:13,14).

It is the Holy Spirit who produces the very character of Jesus in and through you. **But the fruit of the Spirit is love, joy, peace, long-suffering, kindness, goodness, faithfulness, gentleness, self control. Against such there is no law** (Galatians 5:22, 23).

There are two ways to go about living the Christian life. One is to attempt by our own strength to live for Jesus. The other is to allow the Holy Spirit to live the life of Jesus through you! If you *try* in your own ability to produce this fruit of Jesus' character, you will only become frustrated. But if you allow the Holy Spirit to produce His fruit in you, then you will enter into a joyful walk of trusting and yielding to the gracious control of the Holy Spirit.

Not only does the Holy Spirit produce the fruit of Jesus in our lives, He also gifts Christians with special enablements. These gifts of the Spirit are listed in the Bible. Ephesians 4 speaks of specially gifted men whom Jesus has given to the church by His Spirit: apostles, prophets, evangelists, pastors and teachers. Romans 12 describes the spiritual gifts of prophecy, faith, the ministry of helps, teaching, exhortation, giving and mercy.

These gifts are given to Christians today to strengthen the church and give the church supernatural power to build up believers and reach the entire world with the Good News of Jesus Christ.

3

Finding a Local Church Home

Some Christians have spent most of their born-again lives searching for the *perfect* church. No place like that exists. As long as humans make up churches, churches will be less than perfect. However, this is no reason to dismiss the church. The church is ordained and instituted by God Himself. The true church is comprised of all those who have repented of their sins and committed their lives to Jesus Christ. But this global church expresses itself in local, visible groups of believers. The Apostle Paul urged the leaders of the church at Ephesus, **Take heed to yourselves and to all the flock, among which the Holy Spirit has made you overseers, to shepherd the church of God which He purchased with His own blood** (Acts 20:28). Due to the high price that was paid for the church's redemption, the church is of utmost value to God. It should be to you as well.

Your Need for Fellowship

The need for a strong local church in your life cannot be over-emphasized. The day of the Christian who tries to live the Christian life in a vacuum is over.

When you think of *the church,* you should not think of a building, of bricks and mortar. Under the New Covenant, because of the blood of Jesus, redeemed people are the church, not the buildings where they meet. Actually, Christians do not build sanctuaries, we are sanctuaries. God dwells in us by His Spirit.

Or do you not know that your body is the temple of the Holy Spirit who is in you, whom you have from God, and you are not your own? For you were bought at a price; therefore glorify God in your body and in your spirit, which are God's.

1 Corinthians 6:19, 20

We live in a society where people are increasingly becoming *loners.* Jesus predicted this would happen. He said, **And because** lawlessness will abound, the love of many will grow cold (Matthew 24:12). Yet this cannot be tolerated among fervent Christians. We are not allowed the seeming luxury of sealing ourselves away from each other. We need each other.

Till we all come to the unity of the faith and the knowledge of the Son of God, to a perfect man, to the measure of the stature of the fullness of Christ; that we should no longer be children, tossed to and fro and carried about with every wind of doctrine, by the trickery of men, in the cunning craftiness by which they lie in wait to deceive, but speaking the truth in love, may grow up in all things into Him who is the head — Christ — from whom the whole body, joined and knit together by what ever joint supplies, according to the effective working by which every part does its share, causes growth of the body for the edifying of itself in love.

Ephesians 4:13-16

Are you doing your share as part of the body of Christ? It is impossible to sustain a strong love and witness for the Lord without the love and support of His people. Just as one log may burn for a little while, when many logs are put together, they draw warmth from each other and burn even brighter.

The Privilege of Giving

Why should you go to church anyway? To hear the choir sing? To hear the pastor preach? What's the purpose of meeting together?

The primary purpose of meeting corporately is to give, not to get. You will receive blessings from this experience, but that is not the main reason for being a strong, fellowshipping member. The purpose of meeting is giving.

Give, and it will be given to you: good measure, pressed down, shaken together, and running over will be put into your bosom. For with the same

29

measure that you use, it will be mea-
sured back to you.

Luke 6:38

First, you give to the Lord. The Psalmist
said, **Give unto the Lord, O you mighty
ones, Give unto the Lord glory and strength.
Give unto the Lord the glory due to His
name; Worship the Lord in the beauty of
holiness** (Psalm 29:1). You give to the Lord
as you praise His name and worship Him. A
heart of joyful praise should be the trade-
mark of every Christian.

When the church meets, not only do you
give to the Lord, you also give to His people
— your brothers and sisters in Christ. The
closer we get to the return of Christ, so much
more are we to encourage each other by
meeting together publicly to worship the
Lord and be instructed in the Christian walk.

**And let us consider one another in
order to stir up love and good works,
not forsaking the assembling of ourselves together, as is the manner of
some, but exhorting one another, and**

so much the more as you see the Day approaching.

Hebrews 10:24,25

Now you are able to give to the world — to those who so desperately need what we have found in Jesus Christ. Having been nurtured by worship, exhortation from the Word and fellowship with other Christians, you are ready to share the love of Jesus with those who have not yet come to know Him.

What Kind of Church?

One of the most important questions new Christians have is, "What kind of church should I attend? After all, there are so many denominations and independent churches. Which one is the right one?" This is a very legitimate and complex question. Our God is a God of variety. Some churches are seemingly better suited to some people more than others. However, in any church where you identify, there should be at least three distinguishing marks.

1) You should unite with a church where *Jesus Christ is central in all that is said and done.* Unfortunately, this is not the case in every church. The chief identity of some is their own minor doctrine. Don't join in any movement or church that is not first and foremost a Jesus church. Paul said, **For I determined not to know anything among you except Jesus Christ and Him crucified** (1 Corinthians 2:2). Any deviation from the central theme of Jesus Christ should be a danger signal, warning you to keep clear.

2) You should unite with a church where *the Bible is preached as the authoritative Word of God.* Stay away from any group that claims to have *further written revelation* apart from the Bible. Find a church where the Bible is honored as God's love letter to man, truth without any mixture of error.

3) You should unite with a church where you will be *free to worship the Lord in spirit and in truth.* Look for a church that honors the work of the Holy Spirit and allows Him to move freely in their services.

Perhaps your most valuable possession other than your Lord are your brothers and sisters in Christ. You need them. They need you. So, unite with a strong church where Jesus is preached and worshiped as Lord. It's important that you do it now — don't wait!

4

Gaining Understanding
From the Bible

No book in history has influenced lives and nations as has the Bible. George Washington said, "It is impossible rightly to govern without God and the Bible." The United States' ethics and morality are based on the Bible. Our laws stem from the Bible.

However, the Bible is not just the standard for society, it is especially the standard by which Christians are to live.

All Scripture is given by inspiration of God and is profitable for doctrine, for reproof, for correction, for instruction in righteousness, that the man of God may be complete, thoroughly equipped for every good work.

2 Timothy 3:16, 17

In the original language, this verse begins, "All scripture is God-breathed. . ." As the very breathed-out Word of God, we are to heed what the Bible says. We are not to judge the Bible. We are to allow the Bible to judge us. The Bible is God's love letter to you. Through its sacred pages God speaks to you — guiding, warning, correcting, and expressing His love.

What the Bible Is All About

The Bible is comprised of 66 books written by some 40 authors over a span of some 1600 years. Its divine author is the Holy Spirit. **Knowing this first, that no prophecy of Scripture is of any private interpretation, for prophecy never came by the will of man, but holy men of God spoke as they were moved by the Holy Spirit** (2 Peter 1:20, 21). English preacher of the nineteenth century, Charles Spurgeon, said, "The Book is a divine production; it is perfect, and is the last court of appeal — 'the judge which ends all strife.' I would as soon dream of blaspheming my Maker as of questioning the infallibility of His Word."

The central theme of the Bible is redemption. Through its pages run a scarlet thread of redemption as God goes to incredible lengths, even to the sending of His Son to die, so that you can be redeemed and brought back to Him.

The Bible is divided into two sections: the Old Testament and the New Testament. In the Old Testament, the Law and the Prophets pointed to the coming Redeemer who would be sacrificed for man's sinful rebellion. In the New Testament, Jesus of Nazareth is revealed as God's Son, His agent of redemption, who will one day rule planet Earth as King of kings and Lord of lords.

The first five books of the Bible, Genesis through Deuteronomy, are often called Books of the Law. They tell how God created the world, revealed His will by giving the Ten Commandments, and called the children of Israel to be a light to show the one true God to all people.

The Books of History, Joshua through Esther, chronicle Israel's intermittent disobedience and repentance and God's steadfast love toward them. The Books of Poetry, Job through the Song of Solomon, run the gamut of human emotions, showing us God's presence both in times of exhilaration and in times of despair.

The Books of the Prophets, Isaiah through Malachi, record God's prophetic warnings, judgment and tender love toward His people.

The Old Testament is of tremendous value to us today as Christians. In the Old Testament we see God's plan of redemption, progressively being revealed, until it would one day be climaxed as God's Son hung bleeding on a Roman cross. Regarding the Old Testament Scriptures, Paul reminds us, **For whatever things were written before were written for our learning, that we through the patience and comfort of the Scriptures might have hope** (Romans 15:4).

In the New Testament God reveals His New Covenant with man based on the sacrifice of His Son for man's sin. The Gospels, Matthew through John, are error-free, biographical accounts of the life and ministry of Jesus.

The Book of Acts is the historical account of the life of the Early Church. This book is also the pattern for church life today.

The letters to the churches, Romans through Jude, define Christian doctrine and living for us during this Church Age.

The Book of the Revelation is a prophetic look into the future when the earth ultimately comes under the rule of Jesus Christ.

How To Study the Bible

In every book and in every line of Scripture, God desires to speak to you. When you read your Bible, pray that God will open your eyes to His truth for you. Let your prayer be, **Open my eyes, that I may see Wondrous things from Your law** (Psalm 119:18). The line of a great hymn says, "Beyond the sacred page, I seek Thee, Lord." Ask the Lord to reveal Himself to you through His Word.

Come reverently to the Bible. Also, come expectantly. You should expect God to speak to you because this is a living book. **For the word of God is living and powerful, and sharper than any two-edged sword, piercing even to the division of soul and spirit, and of joints and marrow, and is a discerner of the thoughts and intents of the heart** (Hebrews 4:12).

As you meditate on Scripture and obey its truths, God promises to crown your life with success.

This Book of the Law shall not depart from your mouth, but you shall meditate in it day and night, that you may observe to do according to all that is written in it. For then you will make your way prosperous, and then you will have good success.

Joshua 1:8

How To Start

Begin by reading the Gospel of John. As you read, throw away all your preconceptions of Jesus and allow the Holy Spirit to reveal Him to you in a fresh way. You may wish to supplement your reading of John with other portions of Scripture. For instance, if you read five Psalms and one chapter from Proverbs each day, you will complete the book of Psalms and Proverbs in one month. After a year of daily meditation in the Psalms and Proverbs, just watch how your life will begin to change.

After you have read and studied the Gospel of John, read the Book of Romans. It is the clearest and most definitive presentation of the Gospel in the Bible. Perhaps you would want to take one book of the Bible as your life-project, memorizing the entire book and devouring each truth from its pages.

Keep in mind that a quiet place is very helpful as you study. Many people find that the early morning hours are excellent for Bible reading. Others find the lunch hour or the evening better. Whatever is best for you, remember to meditate on the Bible's truths both *day and night.*

Also, keep in mind that a good modern version of the Bible will help you comprehend its truths. In fact, an excellent way to study the Bible is to compare two or three versions as you read. You might even want to start reading the entire Bible each year. Many Bibles contain a chart indicating the most effective way to accomplish this.

Don't forget Scripture memory. Some hostages who were later released have said that their knowledge of God's Word was their most precious asset during their difficult ordeal. In your life as well, nothing is more valuable than your knowledge of the Word of God — and your intimate knowledge of the God of the Word.

Look around you. Everything you see is in the process of wearing away. Everything, that is, except the Word of God.

The grass withers, the flower fades, But the word of our God stands forever.

Isaiah 40:8

5

Developing Your Prayer Life

If the President of the United States requested to see you at the White House, you would spare no expense to meet his request. No matter what it took, you would make that important appointment. Why? Because a man of great authority desires to talk to you. Yet the God of the universe, the King above all kings and the Lord above all lords desires to talk to you! Are you making that appointment? God has invited you to commune with Him.

Prayer is communion with God. In prayer you speak to God about yourself and you speak to God concerning others. There could be no higher privilege on earth than for a mortal man to be ushered into the throneroom of the God of the universe. Because of the blood of Jesus, Christians have this direct access to God anytime, anywhere.

Let us therefore come boldly to the throne of grace, that we may obtain

mercy and find grace to help in time of need.

Hebrews 4:16

Rejoice always, pray without ceasing, in everything give thanks; for this is the will of God in Christ Jesus for you.

1 Thessalonians 5:16-18

Your Hotline to Heaven

You have the possibility of helping to shape the course of human history by your prayers. Yes, you have the opportunity to literally change the world by bringing God's will into effect through prayer. Your own life will be changed by prayer. The lives of your loved ones will be changed and even entire nations can be affected by your prayers.

God gave an incredible promise to those who will be serious concerning this matter of prayer. He said, **Call to Me, and I will answer you, and show you great and mighty things, which you do not know** (Jeremiah 33:3). Are you desiring to see *great and mighty* *things?* They can be yours as you pray.

You literally have a hotline to heaven. Because of the new and living way which Jesus opened for every Christian by His blood, you have direct access to God.

We are to pray for several reasons. For one thing, God urges us to pray. Also, so much good is accomplished through prayer. Alfred Lord Tennyson was right: "More things are wrought through prayer than this world dreams of."

This very moment you, as a Christian, have a privilege only dreamed of by those in former ages. You have direct access to God because of Jesus' blood. By this *new and living way,* you can enter directly into God's presence.

When you pray, it is not necessary to use religious sounding words. In fact, Jesus denounced those who made a show of their prayers and thought that they would be heard *for their much speaking.* Instead of religious oratory, Jesus urged simple, direct prayer to God, even encouraging us to call the Almighty God, *our Father.*

The Lord Jesus offers us spectacular promises of answered prayer when we come to Him in faith using the authority of His name. He said, **And whatever you ask in My name, that I will do, that the Father may be glorified in the Son. If you ask anything in My name, I will do it** (John 14:13, 14). Just think of it! The power of heaven is at your disposal as you pray in Jesus' name!

6

Sharing Your Faith

There is no higher privilege in life than sharing your faith in Christ with others. Jesus has equipped you with His own power for this task. He promised, **But you shall receive power when the Holy Spirit has come upon you; and you shall be witnesses to Me in Jerusalem, and in all Judea and Samaria, and to the end of the earth** (Acts 1:8). He has commanded us to extend our witness for Him to the very extremities of the earth. **Go into all the world and preach the gospel to every creature** (Mark 16:15).

Not only is it your privilege to share the good news of Christ, it is your responsibility. God commands us to warn the wicked to turn from their ways.

When I say to the wicked, "You shall surely die," and you give him no warning, nor speak to warn the wicked from his wicked way, to save his life,

that same wicked man shall die in his iniquity; but his blood I will require at your hand. Yet if you warn the wicked, and he does not turn from his wickedness, nor from his wicked way, he shall die in his iniquity; but you have delivered your soul.

Ezekiel 3:18, 19

You have found the cure for death — tell someone! You have found the cure for sin — a living relationship with Jesus Christ as Savior and Lord. The world has been infested with sin. You have been invested with the cure.

The World Only You Can Reach

You are the only Bible that many people will ever read. Because you are a Christian, whether you like it or not, people are *reading* your life. As they look at you, what do they see? What is the life message you are portraying?

The Apostle Paul said, **For none of us**

lives to himself, and no one dies to himself (Romans 14:7). In other words, your life is affecting the lives of others. Even the least influential person directly affects the lives of others.

You live in concentric circles of relationships with your family, relatives, friends, business acquaintances and others whom you meet. In every relationship you should be concerned to conduct yourself as a worthy ambassador of Jesus Christ. **Therefore we are ambassadors for Christ, as though God were pleading through us: we implore you on Christ's behalf, be reconciled to God** (2 Corinthians 5:20). Remember that your life is pointing people in some direction. Are you pointing them to Jesus?

Are You Qualified?

What are the qualifications to be an effective witness for Jesus Christ?

First, of course, you must have experienced a genuine conversion yourself. You cannot impart what you do not possess. Jesus said, **Out of the abundance of the heart the mouth speaks** (Matthew 12:34). If your heart is filled with Jesus, your mouth will be filled with the message about him.

Second, to be an effective witness for Christ, you must allow the Holy Spirit to control your life. During the dynamic days of growth of the Early Church, multiplied thousands were added to the Lord. This was in direct answer to the prayers of those early Christians for boldness to witness for Christ. After they had prayed for boldness, the Bible says that **the place where they were assembled together was shaken; and they were all filled with the Holy Spirit, and they spoke the word of God with boldness** (Acts 4:31).

You will also experience boldness as you allow the Spirit of God to control your life. If you are in the presence of Jesus, it will be evident to those around you, just as it was evident to those who saw the lives of Peter and John. **Now when they saw the boldness of Peter and John, and perceived that they were uneducated and untrained men, they**

marveled. And they realized that they had been with Jesus (Acts 4:13).

Finally, you must have a love and compassion for people. As you share your faith in Christ, it will be evident to those around you if you genuinely love them. When the devil does not seemingly give way to prayer, he does give way to prayer coupled with tears. **Those who sow in tears Shall reap in joy. He who continually goes forth weeping, Bearing seed for sowing, Shall doubtless come again with rejoicing, Bringing his sheaves with him** (Psalm 126:5,6).

Breaking the Silence Barrier

Why is it easier to talk about every subject under heaven except the subject of heaven — salvation through Jesus Christ? Many times it seems difficult to turn a conversation to spiritual things. Here are a few suggestions on how you can begin to share your faith in Christ with others.

First, share your testimony of how you came to know Christ. You might begin by saying something like this: "May I share with you the most wonderful thing that ever happened to me?" Then proceed to tell the person exactly how you came into a living relationship with Christ. After you have shared your testimony with him, simply ask, "Has this ever happened to you?"

Another way to begin sharing the Gospel is to ask, "Have you ever made the wonderful discovery of knowing Jesus Christ personally?" If the person answers negatively, respond by saying, "You would like to, wouldn't you?" Then proceed to share with him the good news of how Jesus Christ died on the cross for his sins, rose again from the grave, and offers new life to him in this present moment.

Another way to share the love of Christ is to inform the person with whom you are talking about the wonderful things God is doing in your church. If Jesus is manifesting His presence in the congregation, people will want to come experience His life. When Jesus came to Capernaum, . . .it was heard that He **was in the house. Immediately many gath-**

ered together, so that there was no longer room to receive them, not even near the door (Mark 2:1, 2). When you share that *Jesus is in the house*, people will want to come and see what the Lord is doing in your church family.

7

Trust Always In God's Promises

There is no better advice than to trust the promises of God. You can be certain of this: You have come into contact with a trustworthy God. The Bible says that God simply cannot lie. Therefore, you can trust Him implicitly for every circumstance of life.

Because God is trustworthy, His promises to you can be trusted. He will not fail. He cannot fail you. It is impossible for God to lie. It is also impossible for God to fail.

The promises that God has given to Christians in the Bible are magnificent. It is by laying hold of these promises that you come to know God better and actually partake in His life. Peter greeted his fellow believers:

Grace and peace be multiplied to you in the knowledge of God and of Jesus our Lord, as His divine power has given to us all things that pertain to life and godliness, through the knowl-

edge of Him who called us to glory and virtue, by which have been given to us exceedingly great and precious promises, that through these you may be partakers of the divine nature, having escaped the corruption that is in the world through lust.

2 Peter 1:2-4

Peter says that through the *exceedingly great and precious promises* that God has given to you, you come to know Him better and literally share in His life. Therefore it is important for you to know the promises of God and to hold them as your own.

The Promise of His Presence

Jesus promised, **I will never leave you nor forsake you** (Hebrews 13:5). What more wonderful promise could there be? Here lies the basis for your acceptance: Jesus has promised never to leave you.

But not only has He promised to be with you throughout life, He has promised to manifest His presence to you as you praise Him and worship Him. The Bible says that God dwells in the praises of His people. **But You are holy, Who inhabit the praises of Israel** (Psalm 22:3). As you learn to praise Him both personally and corporately with your church family, you will experience His powerful presence.

When you know that the Lord is with you, all of life has a thread of joy running through it. **You will show me the path of life; In Your presence is fullness of joy; At Your right hand are pleasures forevermore** (Psalm 16:11). And even during the toughest hours of your life the Lord has promised that He will not leave you. David said, **Yea, though I walk through the valley of the shadow of death, I will fear no evil. For You are with me. . .** (Psalm 23:4).

Trust His promise to you — the promise of His presence.

The Promise of His Provision

Even from the time of Abraham, God has revealed Himself as the Lord who provides.

Do not look to any human as your primary source of provision. God is your source. He will provide all your needs. He will provide for you physically, financially, emotionally and psychologically. He will certainly provide for you spiritually. **And my God shall supply all your need according to His riches in glory by Christ Jesus** (Philippians 4:19).

The treasury of heaven is full. The resources of heaven will never be bankrupt. You can draw upon God's provision in Christ Jesus for all your needs.

The Promise of His Power

All authority has been given to Me in heaven and on earth. Go therefore and make disciples of all the nations, baptizing them in the name of the Father and of the Son and of the Holy Spirit, teaching them to observe all things that I have commanded you; and lo, I am with you always, even to the end of the age.

Matthew 28:18-20

On the basis of all authority having been given to Him, Jesus commissions you to go into your world and bring those whom you influence to the obedience of faith.

The Lord has not left you comfortless or powerless for this task. He has given His Holy Spirit to equip you for the task. **But you shall receive the power when the Holy Spirit has come upon you; and you shall be witnesses to Me in Jerusalem, and in all Judea and Samaria, and to the end of the earth** (Acts 1:8).

Satan will see to it that you are tempted to sin and tempted to be diverted from your walk with the Lord. However, you have the promise, **No temptation has overtaken you except such as is common to man; but God is faithful, who will not allow you to be tempted beyond what you are able, but with the temptation will also make the way of escape, that you may be able to bear it** (1 Corinthians 10:13).

Jesus Himself has given you, as His follower, power over all of the power of the devil. You are to recognize the fact that Satan is subject to you but you are to rejoice in the fact that salvation is yours through Christ.

Behold, I give you the authority to trample on serpents and scorpions, and over all the power of the enemy, and nothing shall by any means hurt you. Nevertheless do not rejoice in this, that the spirits are subject to you, but rather rejoice because your names are written in heaven.

Luke 10:19, 20

Where do you go from here? Just keep walking with Him, wherever and however He leads. The best counsel is this:

But grow in grace and knowledge of our Lord and Savior Jesus Christ. To Him be the glory both now and forever. Amen.

2 Peter 3:18

The Plan of Salvation

- All people have sinned and are separated from God — Romans 3:23.
- God loves you — Romans 5:8.
- Jesus Christ died to forgive your sins — Romans 6:23.
- You can accept Jesus as your Lord and Savior and know God's love — Romans 10:9,10.

A Prayer for Salvation

Dear Lord Jesus,

I know that I am a sinner and need Your forgiveness. I believe that You died for my sins. I want to turn from my sins. I now invite You to come into my heart and life. I want to trust You as Savior and follow You as Lord, and I receive Your salvation by faith in Jesus' name. Amen.

Date _____ Signature _____

Recommended Reading List

Evidence That Demands a Verdict by Josh McDowell
Here's Life Publishers

Why I Believe by D. James Kennedy
Word, Inc.

How To Give Away Your Faith by Paul E. Little
Intervarsity Press

Know Why You Believe by Paul E. Little
Victor Books

Peace With God by Billy Graham
Word, Inc.

The New Convert's Topical Bible by Mike Murdock
Honor Books

My Utmost for His Highest by Oswald Chambers
Barbour and Co.

Turning Point by Ed Gungor
Harrison House Publishers

Suggested Bible Translations

New International Version

The most commonly used of Bible translations today. Widely accepted for its accuracy and adherence to the original text.

New American Standard Version

Excellent translation that is easy to read and grasp the meaning of the original text.

King James Version

Completed in the 1600s and written in "Old English" (thee, thou, thy. . .) and is still favored by many pastors. Some of the wording may prove difficult for the new Bible reader to understand.

New King James Version

A modern *upgrade* of the King James Version. Old English words have been changed to words more commonly used in modern English.

The Living Bible

A simple Bible paraphrase that is easily read by young and old alike. Offers a refreshing rendering of the Psalms.

To stay *radically saved* in the Lord, you should:

1. Pray and read your Bible daily.
   (2 Timothy 3:16,17)

2. Join, attend and become actively involved in a local church regularly.
   (Hebrews 10:24,25)

3. Fellowship with other Christians.
   (Ephesians 4:13-16)

4. Tell others what Jesus has done for you.
   (Mark 16:15)

Additional copies of this book are available from your local bookstore, the author, or from:

Harrison House
P. O. Box 35035
Tulsa, OK 74153

MINISTRIES

Our objective here at Carman Ministries is to minister to the body of Christ and to see lost souls won to the Lord. All of our concerts are done on a free admission, love offering basis. Also, I personally write a monthly newsletter that goes out to all of our financial supporters. If you wish to be on the Carman Ministries mailing list and be notified of upcoming concerts in your area; or become a supporter and receive our monthly newsletter, write:

Carman Ministries
P. O. Box 5093 • Brentwood, TN 37024-5093
(615) 371-1528 • (615) 371-5128 (fax)

**JOIN US IN WINNING THIS
GENERATION FOR JESUS CHRIST**

Official
R.I.O.T.
Gear

R.I.O.T. Manual	$10.00
CD	$15.00
Cassette	$10.00
Pin	$5.00
Dog Tag	$6.00
T-Shirt	$15.00
Cap	$15.00

Why Are We Calling for a R.I.O.T.?

Webster's Dictionary says a riot is ". . . an unrestrained uproar in a public place." And that is what I desire to see — an unrestrained uproar of the praises of our Lord and Savior Jesus Christ in stadiums, arenas, cities, churches, homes, and individual lives all across America.

R.I.O.T. breaks down in this way:
- Righteous: to conform to the Bible
- Invasion: an armed attack
- Of Truth: the real state of affairs

We are called to go forth in a righteous manner to take the truth of God's Word into our schools, cities, and nation. God's Word and praise are the weapons we need to win the battles before us and to claim our cities, our country, and the world for Jesus Christ.

A Righteous Invasion of Truth is needed all across this country. Will you help us start a riot in your community? Together let's preach it; let's sing it; let's shout it; let's cry it — 'cause desperate times need desperate action, and that means we need a R.I.O.T.!